GETTING TH

MOST OUT OF

ADOBE INDESIGN

JOHN GREY

DISCLAIMER

This book is intended for informational and entertainment purposes only. The author and publisher make no guarantees regarding the accuracy, completeness, applicability, or suitability of its contents for any specific purpose.

The information presented is based on the author's personal experiences, research, and opinions. It is not a substitute for professional advice, and readers are encouraged to consult qualified professionals for guidance tailored to their specific circumstances.

Neither the author nor the publisher shall be held liable for any loss, injury, or damages resulting from the use or application of the information provided in this book. Readers assume full responsibility for any actions taken based on its content.

References to third-party resources, websites, or materials are provided for convenience and do not imply endorsement or responsibility for their content or services. Readers should exercise their own judgment when engaging with external sources.

Thank you for your understanding.

TABLE OF CONTENTS

CHAPTER ONE

INTRODUCTION

1.1 <u>Overview and Purpose</u>

InDesign, developed by Adobe Systems, is a desktop publishing software program utilized for crafting a variety of materials including flyers, brochures, magazines, newspapers, and books. It is favoured by graphic designers, artists, publishers, and marketing professionals for its versatility. InDesign projects can be shared across digital and print platforms seamlessly. Initially part of the Creative Suite, InDesign is now available as a standalone product or through the Adobe Creative Cloud subscription. With its comprehensive set of tools, InDesign empowers users to design visually appealing layouts for both digital and print media. It enables the creation of professional-grade pages suitable for publication in both traditional print and online formats. Adobe InDesign is a software application designed for desktop publishing and page layout. It's a popular tool among graphic designers and production artists who use it to create a wide variety of print and digital media projects. InDesign proves particularly advantageous for publications characterized by multiple pages, layouts that seamlessly integrate text and graphics, and projects rich in content. Here's more detail on the purpose and advantages of Adobe InDesign:

Powerful Design and Layout Tools:

- **Master Pages:** This core feature lets you create a template for recurring elements across your document, like headers, footers, and page numbers.

This ensures consistency and saves time, especially for lengthy projects like magazines or books.

- **Grids and Guides:** InDesign offers a customizable grid system and alignment guides to help you create balanced and visually appealing layouts. These tools ensure your text, images, and other elements are positioned precisely and follow a clear design structure.

- **Typography Control:** InDesign caters to professional typographers with features like OpenType font support, which allows for advanced character sets and stylistic variations. You can also control hyphenation, justification, and spacing for optimal readability and aesthetics.

Streamlined Workflow and Collaboration:

- **Styles and Libraries:** Define paragraph, character, and object styles to maintain consistent formatting throughout your project. These styles can be saved in libraries for easy reuse across different InDesign documents.

- **Seamless Integration:** As mentioned earlier, InDesign integrates smoothly with other Creative Cloud applications. You can place and edit Photoshop images or Illustrator graphics directly within InDesign, eliminating the need to export and import files repeatedly. This fosters a more efficient workflow.

- **Collaboration Features:** InDesign supports collaboration features like cloud document storage and commenting tools. This allows teams to work on projects simultaneously and share feedback efficiently.

Versatility for Various Outputs:

- **Interactive Elements:** InDesign isn't limited to static layouts. You can incorporate interactive elements like buttons, hyperlinks, and slideshows for engaging digital publications like eBooks or online brochures.

- **Advanced Export Options:** InDesign offers a variety of export options tailored to different needs. You can export high-resolution print-ready PDFs for professional printing or create interactive EPUB files for eBooks.

- **Data-Driven Design:** InDesign supports data-driven design workflows, allowing you to import and merge data from external sources to personalize layouts or create dynamic content.

In summary, Adobe InDesign goes beyond basic page layout. It empowers designers with a comprehensive toolbox for creating professional print and digital media, with a focus on efficiency, collaboration, and versatility across various outputs.

1.2 Underline: System Requirements

There are two main sets of system requirements to consider for Adobe InDesign: minimum requirements and recommended specs. Here's a breakdown for both:

Minimum Requirements:

- **Operating System:**
  - Windows: Windows 10 (64-bit version 1909 or later) - LTSC versions are not supported.

- macOS: macOS version 12.0 (Monterey), macOS version 11 (Big Sur), and macOS version 10.15 (Catalina)

- **Processor:**
  - Windows: AMD Athlon® 64 processor or Multicore Intel processor (with 64-bit support)
  - macOS: Multicore Intel processor or Apple silicon/M1 with SSE4.2 or higher SIMD engine

- **RAM:** 4 GB (16 GB recommended)

- **Hard Disk Space:**
  - Windows: 3.6 GB of available hard-disk space (SSD recommended)
  - macOS: 4.5 GB of available hard-disk space

- **Display Resolution:** 1024 x 768 (HiDPI display support recommended)

- **Internet:** An internet connection is required for activation, Adobe ID, and license agreement acceptance.

Recommended Specs:

While the minimum requirements will allow you to run InDesign, for a smooth and efficient experience, Adobe recommends exceeding these specs. Here's what's ideal:

- **Processor:** Latest generation multi-core Intel or AMD processor
- **RAM:** 16 GB or more (especially for complex projects with high-resolution images)
- **Hard Disk Space:** Solid State Drive (SSD) with ample free space for application files and project data.
- **Graphics Card (GPU):** While not mandatory, a dedicated graphics card with at least 2GB of VRAM (Video RAM) can significantly improve performance, especially when working with complex graphics or using GPU-accelerated features.

Additionally, your computer should support OpenGL version 4.0 or greater (for Mac).

Additional Notes:

- It's important to check the latest system requirements on the Adobe website, as they may change with new software updates.

- Remember, these are general recommendations. The specific needs for your workflow will depend on the complexity of your projects and the types of files you typically use.

1.3 Interface Overview

Adobe InDesign's interface provides a workspace for creating and manipulating layouts. Here's a breakdown of the key elements:

1. Application Bar (Top):

- This bar runs horizontally across the top of the window and contains the following:

  - **InDesign Logo:** Click here to access the application menu with options like preferences and recent files.

  - **Menu Bar:** Provides access to various functions categorized by menus like File, Edit, Object, and Text.

  - **Search Bar (Optional):** Search for specific tools, menus, or help content within InDesign.

  - **View Controls:** Zoom in/out, switch between full screen and windowed mode, arrange document windows (tile, cascade).

- o **Workspace Switcher:** Quickly switch between pre-defined workspace layouts optimized for different tasks (e.g., Essentials, Typography).

2. Control Panel (Left):

- This contextual panel changes based on the currently selected tool. It displays options and settings relevant to the chosen tool, allowing you to fine-tune its behaviour.

3. Document Window (Centre):

- This is the main workspace where you create your layout. It displays your document with rulers along the edges (optional) for measurement reference.

4. Toolbar (Left side by default):

- The toolbar contains various tools categorized by function:
  - o Selection tools (e.g., Arrow tool, Direct Selection tool) for selecting and manipulating objects.

- Text tools (e.g., Type tool, Path Text tool) for creating and editing text frames.

- Shape tools (e.g., Rectangle tool, Ellipse tool) to create geometric shapes.

- Pen tool for drawing custom freehand paths.

- Frame tools (e.g., Rectangle Frame tool, Oval Frame tool) for placing images and other content.

5. Panels (Right side):

- The right side of the interface is dedicated to customizable panels that provide access to specific functionalities and information. Some common panels include:

- Layers panel: Manage the stacking order and visibility of elements in your layout.

- Characters panel: Format text properties like font style, size, colour, and spacing.

- Paragraphs panel: Control paragraph settings like alignment, indentation, and justification.

- Swatches panel: Manage and apply colours to your document.

- You can open, close, and rearrange panels to suit your workflow preferences.

Customization:

The beauty of InDesign's interface is its customizability. You can:

- Drag and drop panels to different locations on the screen.

- Group frequently used panels together.

- Save custom workspaces with specific panel layouts for different project types.

By understanding these core interface elements and how to personalize them, you can efficiently create professional layouts in Adobe InDesign.

CHAPTER TWO

GETTING STARTED

2.1 Setting Up a New Document

InDesign offers a flexible approach to setting up new documents. Here's a breakdown of the process:

1. Launching a New Document:

There are two main ways to create a new document in InDesign:

- **File Menu:** Go to **File > New > Document**. This opens the "New Document" dialog box.

- **Welcome Screen:** If it's your first time launching InDesign, you'll see a Welcome Screen. Click on **"Document"** under the "Create New" section.

2. New Document Dialog Box:

This box lets you define various settings for your document:

- **Intent:** Choose the intended purpose of your document (e.g., Print, Web, Video). This selection influences the presets available in other options.

- **Number of Pages:** Specify the number of pages in your document. You can also choose to create "Facing Pages" for layouts like magazines or books.

- **Page Size:** Select a pre-defined page size (e.g., Letter, A4) or define a custom size by entering width and height values.

- **Orientation:** Choose Portrait (tall) or Landscape (wide) orientation for your pages.

- **Margins:** Set the margins around the edge of your page content.

- **Columns:** Define the number of columns you want to use for your layout (optional).

- **Bleed and Slug:** Bleed refers to an area that extends beyond the page size for trimming during printing. Slugs are used for adding private information outside the printable area. (These are typically for advanced users)

3. Presets (Optional):

InDesign offers a variety of document presets depending on the chosen Intent. These presets come with pre-defined settings for page size, margins, and columns, tailored to common project types like flyers, brochures, or social media posts.

4. Setting Up Advanced Options (Optional):

The "New Document" dialog box offers additional options for experienced users, like:

- **Text Frame Padding:** Set the default spacing between text frames and the page margins.

- **Starting Page Number:** Specify the starting page number for your document.

- **Preview:** See a visual preview of your chosen page size and orientation.

5. Click "Create"

Once you've configured the desired settings, click the "Create" button to generate your new InDesign document and start working on your layout!

Additional Tips:

- You can modify most document settings even after creating the document. Use the "Document Setup" dialog box (accessible under the "Layout" menu) to adjust page size, margins, and other properties.

- Consider the bleed area if your project will be printed professionally. Ensure important content stays within the page size and any elements that extend beyond are included in the bleed area.

2.2 Navigation and Zooming

In Adobe InDesign, navigating your document and zooming in and out on specific areas are crucial for working efficiently. Here's a breakdown of the essential techniques:

Navigation:

- **Hand Tool:** This tool (looks like a hand icon) is your primary tool for panning around your document. Click and hold anywhere in the document window, then drag in the desired direction to move your view.

 **Hand (H)**

- **Page Navigation:**

- o **Page Navigator Panel:** This panel (located on the right side by default) displays thumbnails of all your document pages. Click on a thumbnail to jump to that specific page.

- o **Go To Page Menu:** Alternatively, go to the "Pages" menu in the menu bar and select "Go To Page" to enter a specific page number.

- **Keyboard Shortcuts:**

  - o Use the arrow keys on your keyboard to nudge your view slightly up, down, left, or right.

  - o Hold down the Spacebar key and then use the arrow keys to move larger distances.

  - o Press "Page Up" or "Page Down" to jump between pages.

Zooming:

- **Zoom Tool:** This tool (looks like a magnifying glass) is your primary tool for zooming. There are several ways to use it:

  - o Click once on the document window to zoom in to a preset level. Click repeatedly for further magnification.

  - o Hold down the "Option" key (Mac) or "Alt" key (Windows) and click to zoom out.

  - o Click and drag to create a selection box around the area you want to zoom in on. Release the mouse button to zoom in on that specific area.

🔍 Zoom (Z)

- **Keyboard Shortcuts:**
  - Use "Command" or "Control" key (depending on your OS) with "+" or "-" to zoom in or out incrementally.
  - Press "Command" or "Control" key with "0" (zero) to fit the entire page in the document window.
  - Press "Command" or "Control" key with "+" and "Option" or "Alt" key to zoom in proportionally to fit the entire spread (two facing pages) in the window (applicable to multi-page documents).

Additional Tips:

- The zoom level is displayed in the bottom left corner of the document window.

- You can use the "Scrubby Zoom" feature (available in the "GPU Preview" mode) by clicking and dragging up and down in the document window to zoom in and out smoothly.

- Consider using the "Fit Page" or "Fit Spread" options from the "View" menu for quick navigation to different page overviews.

CHAPTER THREE

WORKING WITH OBJECTS

3.1 Creating Shapes and Lines

Adobe InDesign offers a dedicated toolbox for creating various shapes and lines within your document layouts. Here's a rundown of the essential tools and techniques:

1. Shape Tools:

InDesign provides a set of shape tools located on the Toolbar by default. These tools allow you to create basic geometric shapes with ease:

- **Rectangle Tool (M):** Click, hold, and drag to create a rectangle. Hold "Shift" while dragging to constrain the shape to a perfect square.

   Rectangle (M)

- **Ellipse Tool (L):** Similar to the Rectangle tool, click, hold, and drag to create an ellipse. Hold "Shift" for a perfect circle.

   Ellipse (L)

- **Polygon Tool** (This tool might not have a visible icon): Click and drag to create a polygon with a specific number of sides. You can adjust the number of sides and their prominence using the arrow keys while creating the shape. Enter to switch between adjusting sides and corner angles.

 Polygon

2. Pen Tool:

For more complex shapes, the Pen tool offers greater flexibility. It allows you to create custom paths by clicking and dragging to define anchor points and control handles:

- Click to create a corner point. Click and drag to create a curved segment.
- Hold "Shift" while clicking to create straight segments.
- Use the handles extending from corner points to adjust the curvature of your path.

■ ♦ **Pen (P)**

3. Line Tool ():

This tool allows you to draw straight lines. Click once to define the starting point, then click again at the desired endpoint. Hold "Shift" while drawing to constrain the line to a perfect horizontal or vertical line. Additionally, hold "Shift" and "Option/Alt" key together to draw a perfectly straight line from the centre point.

\ **Line (\)**

Additional Tips:

- You can modify the appearance of shapes and lines after creating them:

  - Change fill colour and stroke (outline) using the Swatches panel and the Stroke panel.

  - Adjust stroke weight and linetype (e.g., dashed lines) using the Stroke panel.

  - Resize shapes and lines using the Selection tool and dragging the corner handles.

- Experiment with combining these tools to create more intricate shapes. For instance, you can use the Pen tool to create a custom path and then apply a fill colour to turn it into a unique shape.

By mastering these tools and techniques, you can incorporate various shapes and lines into your InDesign layouts to enhance visual communication and achieve your design goals.

3.2 Manipulating Objects: Transformation, and Alignment

InDesign provides a robust set of tools for manipulating objects within your layouts. Here's a breakdown of essential techniques for transforming and aligning objects:

Transformation:

- **Selection Tool (V):** This is your primary tool for selecting and manipulating objects. Click on an object to select it. Click and hold to select multiple objects (hold "Shift" for individual selection within a group).

■ ⬚ Selection (V, Escape)*

- **Transform Panel:** This panel (located on the right side by default) displays options for transforming selected objects. You can:

    - **Move:** Enter specific values in the X and Y fields to move the object by precise distances.

    - **Scale:** Use the percentage values in the W (Width) and H (Height) fields to proportionally resize the object. Hold "Shift" while scaling to constrain proportions.

    - **Rotate:** Enter a degree value in the Angle field to rotate the object. Hold "Option/Alt" while dragging a corner handle to rotate from the center point.

    - **Shear:** Adjust the H Shear and V Shear values to distort the object horizontally or vertically. (Use sparingly for subtle effects)

- **Free Transform Tool:** Hold down "Command/Control" key (depending on your OS) while clicking and dragging an object's corner handle to transform it proportionally (resize and rotate simultaneously). Hold "Option/Alt" key while dragging to transform from the centre point.

Alignment:

- **Align Panel:** This panel (located on the right side by default) is crucial for aligning multiple objects precisely.

    - Select the objects you want to align.

- In the "Align Objects" section of the panel, choose the desired alignment option (e.g., Left Edges, Right Edges, Top, Centre, Bottom).
- You can also choose to align objects "To Selection" (based on the first selected object) or "To Page" (based on the document margins).

- **Guides and Rulers:** Utilize rulers along the top and left sides of the document window (enable them from the "View" menu) to create horizontal and vertical guides for precise alignment. Drag from the rulers onto the document window to create guides. You can also use the "Smart Guides" feature (enable from the "View" menu) for context-sensitive alignment guides that appear as you move objects.

- **Keyboard Shortcuts:** InDesign offers keyboard shortcuts for quick alignment:
  - Use "Shift" with arrow keys to nudge selected objects by single pixel increments.
  - Use "Ctrl/Command" with arrow keys to move objects in larger increments.

Additional Tips:

- Group objects together (select objects and right-click > Group) to manipulate them as a single unit while maintaining their relative positions.

- Leverage the "Lock" options in the Layers panel to lock specific object properties (e.g., position, size) to prevent accidental changes.

- Combine these techniques for efficient and precise manipulation of objects in your InDesign layouts.

By mastering these transformation and alignment tools, you can achieve a well-organized and visually balanced layout in your InDesign projects.

3.3 Using Layers for Organization

Layers in Adobe InDesign function similarly to layers in other design software like Photoshop. They provide a hierarchical way to organize and manage the various elements within your document, offering several advantages:

Benefits of Using Layers:

- **Improved Organization:** Complex layouts often involve numerous elements like text frames, images, shapes, and lines. Layers allow you to categorize these elements logically. For example, you might have a separate layer for "Background Images," another for "Text Boxes," and another for "Decorative Lines." This visual organization makes it easier to find, select, and modify specific elements within your design.

- **Selective Editing:** With layers, you can temporarily hide or lock certain layers while editing others. This prevents accidental modifications and streamlines your workflow. Imagine working on text content while temporarily hiding background elements to avoid visual clutter.

- **Version Control and Experimentation:** You can create duplicate layers to experiment with different design variations. This allows you to compare options or revert to previous iterations without affecting the main layout.

Working with Layers in InDesign:

- **Layers Panel:** The Layers panel (located on the right side by default or accessible through the "Window" menu) displays a stacked list representing your document's layers.

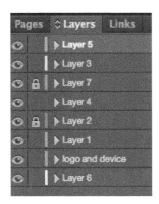

- **Creating Layers:** Click the "+" button at the bottom of the Layers panel to create a new layer. You can also right-click on an existing layer and choose "New Layer" or "Duplicate Layer" from the context menu.

- **Arranging Layers:** Click and drag layers up or down in the Layers panel to change their stacking order. Elements in higher layers appear on top of elements in lower layers, mimicking a real-world stack.

- **Layer Options:** Right-click on a layer to access a context menu with various options:

  - **Rename Layer:** Assign a descriptive name to your layer for better identification within the project.

  - **Lock Layer:** Prevent accidental selection or modification of objects within that layer.

  - **Show/Hide Layer:** Make a layer visible or invisible in the document window without deleting it.

- **Sublayers:** You can create sublayers by dragging a layer on top of another layer and holding it for a moment. This creates a hierarchical relationship, allowing you to further organize elements within a specific layer category.

Additional Tips:

- Use layer colours to visually distinguish different layer groups in the Layers panel.

- Lock the "Background" layer by default to prevent accidental modifications to the document background.

- Take advantage of keyboard shortcuts for faster layer management (consult InDesign's documentation for specific shortcuts).

By effectively using layers, you can maintain a well-organized and manageable workspace, especially when working on intricate InDesign projects.

CHAPTER FOUR

TEXT AND TYPOGRAPHY

4.1 Formatting Text

InDesign offers comprehensive tools for formatting text, allowing you to control the appearance and style of your written content. Here's a breakdown of the key aspects of text formatting:

Character Formatting:

- Character formatting applies to individual characters or a selected range of text within a text frame. You can modify:

    - **Font:** Choose from a vast library of fonts installed on your system.

    - **Font Size:** Specify the desired size for your text in points (pt).

    - **Font Style:** Apply styles like bold, italic, underline, or small caps.

    - **Fill Colour:** Set the text colour using the Swatches panel.

    - **Character Spacing:** Adjust the spacing between individual characters (tracking) or kerning (adjusting space between specific letter pairs).

- **Character Panel:** This panel (located on the right side by default) provides centralized access to all character formatting options. You can directly modify settings or create and apply custom character styles for consistent formatting throughout your document.

Paragraph Formatting:

- Paragraph formatting applies to an entire paragraph or a selected range of paragraphs within a text frame. You can control:

    - **Alignment:** Left-align, right-align, centre-align, or justify your text.

    - **Indentation:** Set the amount of indentation from the left or right margins.

    - **Line Spacing:** Adjust the space between lines of text (leading).

    - **Hyphenation:** Control how InDesign automatically hyphenates words at the end of lines.

- o **Tabs and Spacing:** Set custom tab stops and spacing before and after paragraphs.

- **Paragraphs Panel:** Similar to the Character panel, this panel (also on the right side) offers centralized control over paragraph formatting options. You can create and apply custom paragraph styles for consistent formatting.

OpenType Features (Optional):

InDesign supports advanced OpenType fonts that offer stylistic variations and special characters beyond basic formatting. You can access these features through the Character panel or the dropdown menu within the text frame itself. These features can include:

- **Ligatures:** Ornamental combinations of certain letters for a more aesthetically pleasing look.
- **Swash Caps:** Decorative variations of capital letters.

- **Small Caps:** Capital letters set at a reduced size, often used for emphasis within lowercase text.

Additional Tips:

- Use keyboard shortcuts for faster formatting (consult InDesign's documentation for specific shortcuts).

- Master Styles for ultimate efficiency. Create and apply character and paragraph styles to maintain consistency across your document and easily modify formatting across multiple elements.

- Take advantage of InDesign's built-in spell checker and hyphenation tools to ensure error-free and professional-looking text.

By mastering these formatting techniques, you can transform plain text into visually appealing and well-structured content within your InDesign layouts.

4.2 Paragraph and Character Styles

Paragraph and Character Styles are powerful features in Adobe InDesign that streamline your workflow and ensure consistent formatting throughout your document. Here's a deep dive into their functionalities:

Understanding the Difference:

- **Character Styles:** Apply formatting to specific characters or a selected range of text. This could include font, size, colour, and other character-specific attributes.

- **Paragraph Styles:** Apply formatting to entire paragraphs. This encompasses alignment, indentation, spacing, justification, and other paragraph-level properties.

Benefits of Using Styles:

- **Consistency:** Styles guarantee that all elements formatted with the same style will look identical, maintaining a uniform appearance throughout your document. This is especially crucial for lengthy projects with repetitive formatting needs.
- **Efficiency:** Creating and applying styles saves time compared to manually formatting each text element individually. You can update a style once, and all elements linked to that style will reflect the change instantly.
- **Flexibility:** You can easily modify existing styles to create variations. For instance, you might have a "Body Text" style and create a "Subheading" style based on it, changing the font size and adding bold formatting.
- **Organization:** Styles are displayed in the Paragraph Styles and Character Styles panels, providing a clear overview of all your formatting presets within the document.

Creating and Applying Styles:

1. **Select the text:** Choose the text you want to base your style on (for character styles) or the entire paragraph (for paragraph styles).

2. **Open the Styles Panel:** Go to "Window" > "Styles" to open the Paragraph Styles panel (for paragraph styles) or the Character Styles panel (for character styles).

3. **Create a New Style:**

   o **Character Styles:** Click the "Create New Character Style" button (looks like a small paragraph symbol with a plus sign) at the bottom of the Character Styles panel.

   o **Paragraph Styles:** Click the "Create New Paragraph Style" button (looks like a paragraph symbol with a plus sign) at the bottom of the Paragraph Styles panel.

4. **Edit Style Properties (Optional):** In the "New Paragraph Style" or "New Character Style" dialog box, you can modify various formatting options depending on the style type.

5. **Name Your Style:** Assign a descriptive name to your style for easy identification within the panels.

6. **Apply the Style:** Select the text elements where you want to apply the style. Then, click on the desired style name in the Paragraph Styles or Character Styles panel.

Additional Tips:

- **Base Styles:** Create a "Base Style" with your core formatting preferences and use it as a foundation for other styles. This ensures consistency across all your derived styles.

- **Style Options:** Explore the advanced options available within the style definition dialog boxes. You can control nesting of styles, hidden characters, and even specify optical margin alignment for improved readability.
- **Style Libraries:** Save and share frequently used styles across different InDesign projects by creating style libraries. This ensures a consistent design language across your work.

By mastering Paragraph and Character Styles, you'll significantly enhance your efficiency and maintain a professional and visually cohesive look in your InDesign layouts. They are essential tools for any designer working with text-heavy documents.

4.3 Advanced Typography Features

InDesign goes beyond basic formatting, offering advanced typography features that cater to professional designers and typographers. Here's a glimpse into some of these features:

OpenType Expertise:

- **Ligatures and Swashes:** As mentioned earlier, InDesign supports OpenType fonts that provide stylistic alternatives like ligatures (combined characters) and swashes (ornate variations of capital letters) for a more polished look.
- **Stylistic Sets:** Some OpenType fonts offer multiple stylistic sets within a single font family. These sets can include variations like small caps, oldstyle figures, or stylistic alternates for specific characters. You can access and

apply these sets through the Character panel or the dropdown menu within the text frame.

Advanced Character Controls:

- **Baseline Shift:** Fine-tune the vertical positioning of individual characters relative to the baseline. This can be helpful for adjusting diacritics (accents) or aligning specific characters with graphic elements.

- **Superscript and Subscript:** Format text as superscript (raised) or subscript (lowered) for mathematical expressions, chemical formulas, or footnotes.

- **Tracking and Kerning:** Control the spacing between characters. Tracking adjusts the spacing uniformly across a selected text range, while kerning allows for fine-tuning the space between specific letter pairs for optimal aesthetics.

Optical Margin Alignment:

This feature refines the alignment of text along the left and right margins. It considers the shapes of characters to create a more visually balanced look, especially for justified text.

Hyphenation Control:

InDesign offers granular control over hyphenation. You can specify hyphenation zones (areas where InDesign can or cannot hyphenate words) and define exceptions for specific words to prevent undesirable hyphenation.

Drop Caps and Ornaments:

Create large, decorative first letters (drop caps) or incorporate typographic ornaments and spacers to enhance the visual appeal of your text. You can customize the size, position, and even source text frame for your drop cap.

Integration with Other Creative Cloud Apps:

- **Content Collector (InCopy):** InDesign integrates with InCopy, allowing multiple writers to collaborate on text content within a central InDesign document.

- **Paragraph Styles from Microsoft Word:** Import paragraph styles from Microsoft Word documents to maintain some formatting consistency when working with transferred content.

Additional Tips:

- Experiment with these features to create unique typographic effects and enhance the visual hierarchy of your layouts.

- Use them sparingly to avoid overwhelming the reader. Maintain a balance between creativity and readability.

- Consult InDesign's documentation or online resources for detailed explanations and tutorials on using these advanced features effectively.

By mastering these advanced typography features, you can elevate the visual impact of your text in InDesign projects, creating layouts that are not only informative but also aesthetically captivating.

CHAPTER FIVE

IMAGES AND GRAPHICS

5.1 Importing Images and Graphics

InDesign excels at integrating visual content alongside text to create compelling layouts. Here's a breakdown of the methods for importing images and graphics into your InDesign document:

1. Placing Images with the "Place" Command:

- This is the primary method for importing images. Go to "File" > "Place" in the menu bar.

- A "Place" dialog box will appear. Navigate to the location of your image file on your computer.

- You can select multiple image files at once for batch importing.

- In the dialog box, you have options to:

  o **Link or Embed:** Linking maintains a connection to the original image file. Embedding incorporates the image data within the InDesign document itself.

  o **Show Import Options:** This opens a menu with settings like scaling, cropping, and colour mode conversion (if applicable).

- Click "Open" to place the image.

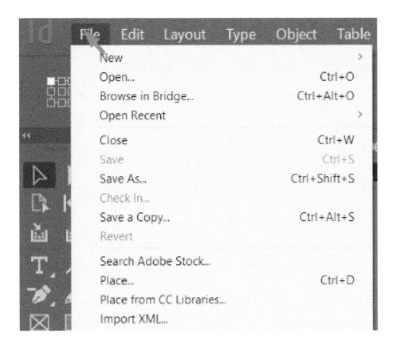

2. Drag-and-Drop Method:

- This is a quicker option for experienced users.

- Navigate to the folder containing your image file on your computer.

- Drag the image file directly onto your InDesign document window.

- InDesign will automatically create a frame around the image and place it.

3. Content Libraries (Optional):

- If you're using Adobe Creative Cloud, you can leverage the built-in Content Libraries (accessible through the Libraries panel).

- Search for and import stock photos, illustrations, and other graphic assets directly from Adobe Stock or other libraries you've subscribed to.

4. Placing EPS (Encapsulated PostScript) Files:

- InDesign can import EPS files, a vector graphics format commonly used for illustrations or logos.

- Placing an EPS file follows the same workflow as placing images, but you might have additional import options specific to vector graphics.

5. Considerations for Different Image Formats:

- InDesign supports various image formats like JPEG, PNG, TIFF, and PSD (Photoshop).

- Choose the appropriate format based on your image type and needs. For instance, JPEGs are suitable for photos with good compression, while PNGs are better for graphics with transparency.

Additional Tips:

- Before placing images, ensure they are sized appropriately for your layout to avoid quality loss due to resizing within InDesign.

- Use the "Content Collector" libraries within InDesign to manage and share graphic assets with team members working on the same project (requires additional setup).

- Explore the "Place Gun" tool (accessible under the "Window" menu) for a more streamlined way to browse and place multiple images at once.

By mastering these image import techniques, you can efficiently integrate visuals into your InDesign projects, enriching your layouts and enhancing communication through impactful design.

5.2 Editing and Adjusting Images within InDesign

While InDesign isn't a full-fledged image editing software like Adobe Photoshop, it offers a surprising amount of control over how you can edit and adjust images placed within your layouts. Here's a breakdown of the key functionalities:

Basic Adjustments:

- **Image Fitting:** Right-click on the image and choose "Fitting" from the context menu. You'll find options to:
  - **Fit Frame:** Resize the image proportionally to fit within the existing frame.
  - **Fill Frame:** Resize the image to fill the entire frame, potentially cropping excess content.
  - **Fit Content to Frame:** Resize the frame itself to snugly fit the image proportions.
- **Image Crop Tool:** Select the image frame and activate the Crop tool (located in the Toolbar by default). Drag the handles on the frame to define the cropping area. Click "Enter" or "Return" to apply the crop.
- **Brightness & Contrast:** Open the "Control" panel (right side by default) and locate the "Brightness" and "Contrast" sliders. Adjust these to enhance or reduce the overall lightness and darkness of the image within the frame.
- **Colour Balance:** The "Control" panel also offers a "Colour Balance" section. Use the sliders to adjust the balance of red, green, and blue tones in the image, potentially correcting colour casts or achieving creative effects.

Advanced Adjustments (Limited):

- **Hue/Saturation:** While InDesign has limited control, you can adjust the overall hue (colour tint) and saturation (intensity of colour) of the image using the sliders in the "Control" panel.

Applying Effects (Limited):

- **Drop Shadow and Inner Shadow:** InDesign allows applying basic drop shadow and inner shadow effects to your placed images. These can add depth and dimension to your layout. You'll find these options in the "Control" panel.

Additional Tips:

- Remember, extensive image editing is best done in Photoshop before placing the image into InDesign.

- Use InDesign's adjustments sparingly to enhance the image within the context of your layout, but avoid overly manipulating the original content.

- Consider using layer masks within Photoshop to create specific areas of transparency or selectively apply adjustments to portions of your image before placing it in InDesign.

By understanding these editing and adjustment options, you can effectively integrate images into your InDesign projects while maintaining basic control over their appearance within your layouts. For in-depth image manipulation, rely on Photoshop and leverage the power of placed, linked images for a streamlined workflow.

5.3 Working with Vector Graphics

InDesign excels at integrating not only raster images (photos) but also vector graphics into your layouts. Vector graphics, unlike raster images, are resolution-independent and composed of paths and strokes. This means they can be scaled to any size without losing quality, making them ideal for logos, icons, and other scalable design elements. Here's a primer on working with vector graphics in InDesign:

Importing Vector Graphics:

- There are two primary methods for incorporating vector graphics into your InDesign document:

  - **Placing AI, EPS, or PDF Files:** These are common file formats for vector graphics created in Adobe Illustrator or other vector design software. Follow the same process as importing images using the "Place" command (File > Place). When placing, you can choose to link or embed the vector graphic file.

  - **Using the InDesign Shape Tools:** While InDesign isn't a full-fledged vector illustration application, it offers basic shape tools that allow you to create simple geometric shapes (rectangles, circles, polygons) and lines. You can then manipulate these shapes using the Pathfinder panel (similar to the Pathfinder panel in Illustrator) to combine, subtract, or intersect shapes, creating more complex vector elements directly within InDesign.

Editing and Manipulating Vector Graphics (Placed or Created):

- Once you have a vector graphic in your InDesign document, you can manipulate it in several ways:

  - **Transform Panel:** Use the Transform panel (right side by default) to scale, rotate, or move the vector graphic. Remember, vector graphics can be scaled infinitely without quality loss.

- o **Stroke and Fill Properties:** Double-click the vector graphic to open the "Object Style Options" dialog. Here, you can modify the fill colour, stroke colour, stroke weight, and other visual properties of the vector graphic.

- o **Pathfinder Panel (Limited):** InDesign offers a limited version of the Pathfinder panel, allowing you to perform basic boolean operations like uniting, excluding, or intersecting overlapping shapes. This can be useful for combining or modifying the paths of your vector graphics.

Additional Tips:

- If you need extensive editing capabilities for your vector graphics, it's recommended to create or modify them in Adobe Illustrator before placing them into InDesign.

- InDesign offers an "Edit Original" option (right-click on the placed vector graphic) that allows you to open the graphic directly in Illustrator for advanced editing. Once you save the changes in Illustrator, the linked vector graphic in InDesign will update automatically.

- Consider using a combination of InDesign's shape tools and placed vector graphics from Illustrator for a more efficient workflow.

By understanding these methods for working with vector graphics, you can leverage their scalability and flexibility to enhance your InDesign layouts with high-quality, resolution-independent design elements.

CHAPTER SIX

LAYOUT AND DESIGN PRINCIPLES

6.1 Grids, Guides, and Margins

InDesign utilizes grids, guides, and margins to establish a structured foundation for your layouts. These elements help you achieve consistent spacing, alignment, and organization within your document.

Grids:

- A grid system acts as a barely visible background of horizontal and vertical lines that segment your document area. It serves as a guide for placing text frames, images, and other design elements.

- **Creating a Grid:**

  o Go to **Layout** menu > **Margins and Columns**.

  o In the "Margins and Columns" dialog box, switch to the **Grids** tab.

  o You can define the number of horizontal and vertical lines (divisions) you want in your grid.

  o Choose the spacing between grid lines (gutter) and set the grid's starting position (margins).

  o Click **OK** to create the grid.

- **Using the Grid:**

  o The grid itself won't be printed. It's a visual reference for aligning objects and maintaining consistent spacing throughout your design.

- InDesign offers "Snap to Grid" functionality (found under the **View** menu). When enabled, objects will automatically nudge to align with the grid lines as you move them, ensuring precise placement.

Guides:

- Guides are individual horizontal or vertical lines that you can create and position anywhere on your document page. Unlike the grid, they are more prominent and customizable.

- **Creating Guides:**

  - You can drag horizontal guides from the ruler at the top of the document window.

  - Drag vertical guides from the ruler on the left side of the document window.

  - You can also use the **Pen Tool** (hold **Shift** for straight lines) to create guides directly on the artboard.

- **Using Guides:**

  - Guides are helpful for aligning objects to specific positions within your layout. You can use them to create margins, section dividers, or baselines for text frames.

  - Objects will also snap to guides when the "Snap to Guides" option is enabled under the **View** menu.

Margins:

- Margins define the space between the edge of the page and the content area of your document. They provide a buffer zone to enhance readability and visual balance.

- **Setting Margins:**
  - The same **Margins and Columns** dialog box used for grids also allows you to set margins.
  - In the dialog box, enter the desired spacing values for the top, bottom, left, and right margins of your document.
  - Margins are crucial for ensuring your content doesn't touch the very edge of the page, especially when considering potential bleed areas for printing.

Using Grids, Guides, and Margins Together:

These elements work cohesively to establish a structured layout. The grid provides a background framework, while guides offer more specific alignment references. Margins define the overall content area within the page boundaries.

By effectively combining these tools, you can achieve a well-organized, professional-looking design in your InDesign projects. They streamline the layout process and ensure consistency in the placement of your design elements.

6.2 Page Numbering and Sections

InDesign offers powerful tools for managing page numbering and document sections. These features are essential for creating paginated documents like brochures, magazines, or books.

Page Numbering Basics:

- **Automatic Page Numbering:** InDesign allows you to insert page numbers automatically onto your document pages.

- **Master Pages:** Page numbering is typically applied on master pages. These are special layout templates that act as a blueprint for your document's regular pages. Elements placed on a master page will be replicated across all pages based on that master.

Inserting Page Numbers:

1. **Open the Pages Panel:** Go to **Window** > **Pages**.

2. **Double-Click a Master Page:** Select the master page where you want to insert page numbers (usually the right or left-facing page depending on your document setup).

3. **Create a Text Frame:** Use the Text Frame tool to create a small text box on the master page where you want the page number to appear.

4. **Insert Special Character:** Click inside the text frame and go to **Type** > **Insert Special Character** > **Markers** > **Current Page Number**. This will insert a placeholder that will automatically display the page number on each document page linked to this master.

5. **Format the Page Number:** You can style the page number using the Character panel (font, size, color). You can also add prefixes or suffixes (e.g., "Page " or "Chapter 1 - ").

Multiple Page Numbering Systems (Optional):

InDesign allows for more complex numbering schemes. You can create different numbering styles (e.g., Roman numerals for introductory pages, Arabic numerals for the main content) and apply them to specific page ranges or sections within your document.

Using Sections:

- Sections are logical divisions within your document. They allow for independent page numbering and formatting for different parts of your project.

- **Creating Sections:**
    - Go to a page where you want to start a new section.
    - Right-click on the page number (or the page itself if no number is present) and choose **Numbering & Section Options**.
    - In the dialog box, check the **Start New Section** box. You can also define a section name for better organization.

- **Benefits of Sections:**
    - Independent Page Numbering: You can define different numbering styles (starting numbers, prefixes) for each section.
    - Restarting Page Numbers: For example, you might want the introduction to start with Roman numerals (e.g., "Preface - i") and then switch to Arabic numerals (e.g., "1") for the main content. Sections allow you to achieve this.
    - Different Formatting: You can apply different master pages or layout styles to different sections of your document.

Additional Tips:

- Use the "Show Text Threads" option under the **View** menu to visualize the connection between page numbers on your master pages and their instances on document pages.

- Leverage InDesign's ability to synchronize numbering across different sections. This ensures automatic updates if you add or remove pages within your document.

- Explore nested sections for even more intricate numbering control within complex documents.

By mastering page numbering and sections, you can streamline your workflow, maintain consistent numbering throughout your InDesign projects, and create professional-looking paginated documents.

6.3 Master Pages and Templates

Master pages and templates are fundamental concepts in InDesign that empower you to design efficiently and maintain consistency across your documents. Here's a breakdown of their functionalities:

Master Pages:

- Master pages act as reusable layout templates within your InDesign document. Elements placed on a master page are automatically replicated onto all pages linked to that master.

- **Common Uses of Master Pages:**
  - Headers and Footers: Create consistent headers and footers containing page numbers, logos, or other recurring design elements across your document.

- o Background Elements: Apply background colours, textures, or images to all pages using the master page.

- o Document Margins: Define consistent margins for your entire document by setting them on the master page.

- o Branding Elements: Include logos, website URLs, or other branding elements consistently throughout your document.

- **Benefits of Using Master Pages:**

  - o Efficiency: Modifying an element on the master page instantly updates it on all linked pages, saving you time and effort.

  - o Consistency: Ensures a uniform look and feel across your document by maintaining consistent design elements on the master page.

  - o Organization: Keeps your document clutter-free by centralizing recurring elements on the master page.

Creating and Using Master Pages:

- **InDesign creates two default master pages (A-Master and B-Master) by default.** You can add more if your document requires different layouts for specific sections (e.g., left-facing and right-facing pages for a book).

- **The Pages Panel:** The Pages panel (**Window > Pages**) displays thumbnails of all your document's pages, including the master pages.

- **Editing Master Pages:** Double-click on a master page thumbnail to enter editing mode. Here you can place text frames, images, shapes, and lines to define the elements that will be replicated on linked pages.

- **Assigning Master Pages:** In the Pages panel, you can drag and drop a master page thumbnail onto a document page thumbnail to link them. You can also right-click on a page thumbnail and choose "Apply Master" to assign a specific master page.

Templates:

InDesign templates take the concept of master pages a step further. They are pre-designed InDesign documents that serve as a starting point for new projects. Templates typically include:

- Pre-defined master pages with established layouts and styles.
- Placeholder text frames and image frames for easy content population.
- Colour swatches, paragraph styles, and character styles for consistent formatting.
- **Benefits of Using Templates:**
  - Streamlined Workflow: Templates provide a ready-made foundation, allowing you to focus on content creation rather than layout design from scratch.
  - Brand Consistency: Templates ensure consistent branding elements and design styles across all your projects derived from that template.
  - Time-Saving: Eliminate repetitive layout tasks by using pre-designed templates.
- **Creating and Sharing Templates:** You can save a document as a template (**.indt**) after setting up your master pages, styles, and desired

layout. Share these templates with your team or across projects to maintain design consistency.

In Conclusion:

Master pages and templates are powerful tools that empower you to create professional-looking InDesign documents efficiently. By leveraging these features, you can save time, ensure consistency, and establish a streamlined workflow for your design projects.

CHAPTER SEVEN

INTERACTIVE AND DIGITAL PUBLISHING

7.1 Creating Interactive PDFs

InDesign allows you to create interactive PDFs, adding a layer of engagement and dynamic features to your static documents. Here's a breakdown of the key elements involved:

Exporting Interactive PDFs:

- While creating your InDesign document, keep in mind the interactive elements you want to include.

- Once your design is finalized, go to **File > Export**.

- In the **Export** dialog box, choose **Adobe PDF (Interactive)** from the format dropdown menu.

- This activates the **Interactive** settings section within the dialog box.

Interactive Elements:

InDesign offers a variety of interactive features you can embed within your PDF:

- **Buttons and Forms:** Create clickable buttons that can trigger various actions when clicked, such as:

    o Go to a different page within the PDF.

    o Open an external web link.

    o Play a media clip (audio or video).

    o Submit form data (requires further setup with actions).

- **Hyperlinks:** Add hyperlinks to text or images that link to other locations within the PDF, external websites, or email addresses.

- **Multimedia:** Embed multimedia elements like audio clips or video files that can be played directly within the PDF.

- **Comments and Notes:** Allow users to add comments or notes to specific areas of the PDF (requires setting up document permissions).

Setting Up Actions (Optional):

For advanced interactivity, you can define actions that are triggered by user interactions with buttons or form elements. Actions can perform various tasks, such as:

- Changing the view of the PDF (zoom, scrolling).

- Hiding or showing specific document layers.

- Submitting form data to a server (requires additional configuration).

Additional Considerations:

- **Accessibility:** Ensure your interactive PDF elements are accessible to users with disabilities. Consider using clear and descriptive labels for buttons and links.

- **File Size:** Embedding multimedia elements can increase the file size of your interactive PDF. Optimize media files for web delivery if necessary.

- **Testing:** Thoroughly test your interactive PDF to ensure all elements function as intended across different viewing platforms.

Resources:

- InDesign provides detailed documentation and tutorials on creating interactive PDFs. You can access these resources within the application or through Adobe's online help centre.

- There are also many third-party resources and plugins available online that can extend InDesign's interactive capabilities.

By incorporating these elements and considerations, you can transform your InDesign documents into engaging and interactive experiences for your readers. Interactive PDFs can be a valuable tool for presentations, reports, e-learning materials, and more.

7.2 Exporting for Web and Mobile Devices

InDesign, while primarily designed for print layouts, offers functionalities for exporting content optimized for web and mobile devices. Here's a breakdown of the key aspects:

Exporting Options:

- InDesign doesn't directly create responsive web pages or mobile apps. However, it allows you to export your designs in formats suitable for further development or integration into web and mobile projects.

- **Common Export Formats:**
  - **JPEG (.jpg):** A widely used image format with good compression for photos and illustrations, but not ideal for text-heavy content due to potential quality loss.

- **PNG (.png):** Supports transparency and offers better quality for graphics with text or intricate details. Consider using PNG-8 for smaller file sizes when transparency is not crucial.

- **SVG (.svg):** Scalable Vector Graphics format ideal for logos, icons, and other vector elements. SVGs can be resized without losing quality and can also be interactive in web development.

Optimizing for Web and Mobile:

- **Resolution:** Consider the target screen resolutions of web and mobile devices. Exporting images at excessively high resolutions will result in large file sizes that can slow down web page loading times.

- **Image Size and Compression:** Balance image quality with file size. Tools like Adobe Photoshop offer options for optimizing image file sizes for web delivery while maintaining acceptable visual quality.

- **Slicing and Multi-State Objects (Optional):** For complex layouts or user interface elements, you can slice your InDesign artwork into separate image files or create multi-state objects (e.g., button hover states) that can be used in web development workflows.

Beyond InDesign:

- InDesign serves as a design and layout tool. To create fully functional web pages or mobile apps, you'll need to use additional tools and languages like HTML, CSS, and potentially JavaScript depending on the desired level of interactivity.

- Exported assets from InDesign (images, SVGs) can be integrated into web development workflows or used within website builder platforms that offer design and layout functionalities.

Additional Tips:

- **Work with Web Developers:** If you lack web development expertise, collaborate with web developers to ensure your InDesign assets are implemented correctly within web pages or mobile apps.

- **Explore Web Design Tools:** Consider using web design tools like Adobe XD or Figma alongside InDesign for a more comprehensive web design workflow, especially for creating interactive prototypes.

- **Test on Different Devices:** Always test your exported content on various devices and screen sizes to ensure optimal display and functionality.

By understanding these export options and limitations, you can effectively leverage InDesign's strengths for designing visual assets that can be integrated into web and mobile development projects. Remember, InDesign excels at creating layouts, but additional tools and expertise might be needed for full web or mobile app development.

CHAPTER EIGHT

TABLES, CHARTS, AND DATA VISUALIZATION

8.1 Creating and Formatting Tables

InDesign offers a robust set of features for creating and formatting tables, allowing you to present information in a clear, organized, and visually appealing way. Here's a breakdown of the essential steps involved:

Creating a Table:

There are two main methods for creating a table in InDesign:

1. **Using the Text Tool:**

   o Select the Text tool from the toolbar.

   o Click and drag on your document to create a text frame of the desired size for your table.

   o Go to the **Table** menu and choose **Insert Table**.

2. **Using the Table Frame Tool:**

   o Select the **Table Frame Tool** from the toolbar (looks like a grid icon).

   o Click and drag on your document to define the dimensions of your table (number of rows and columns).

Specifying Rows and Columns:

- In both methods, a dialog box will appear after initiating table creation.

- Here, you can specify the exact number of rows (horizontal) and columns (vertical) you need for your table.

- You can also choose to include header and footer rows for separate headers or summaries within your table.

Entering Data:

- Once you have your table frame created, you can start entering your data into the cells.

- Click inside a cell and type your text content.

Formatting Basics:

- InDesign offers various formatting options to customize the appearance of your table:

  - **Cell Text Formatting:** Apply text formatting like font style, size, and colour to the table data using the Character panel or paragraph styles.

  - **Borders and Fills:** Define the line style, weight, and colour of table borders. You can also set fill colours for individual cells or the entire table.

  - **Alignment:** Control the horizontal and vertical alignment of text within table cells. Align text to the left, right, or centre.

  - **Cell Size and Spacing:** Resize table cells by dragging the borders between cells. You can also adjust row and column spacing for better readability.

Advanced Formatting (Optional):

InDesign offers additional features for more intricate table formatting:

- **Merging and Splitting Cells:** Combine or separate cells to create a customized table structure.

- **Cell Styles:** Create reusable cell styles with predefined formatting settings to maintain consistency throughout your tables.

- **Sorting and Filtering (Limited):** Sort table rows alphabetically or numerically based on specific columns.

Tips for Effective Tables:

- **Clarity and Readability:** Prioritize clear presentation of information. Use appropriate font sizes, contrasting colours, and sufficient spacing for easy reading.

- **Visual Hierarchy:** Use bold fonts or headers to highlight important information within the table.

- **Alignment and Consistency:** Maintain consistent formatting across your tables for a professional look.

- **Consider Complexity:** If your table data is very complex, explore alternative ways to present the information, such as charts or graphs, to avoid overwhelming readers.

By mastering these steps and keeping these tips in mind, you can create well-formatted and informative tables that enhance your InDesign document's clarity and professionalism.

8.2 Adding Charts and Infographics

While InDesign isn't built for creating charts and infographics from scratch like a dedicated application such as Adobe Illustrator, it offers a few methods to incorporate them into your layouts:

1. Importing Charts from Other Applications:

- The most common approach is to create your charts and infographics in software like Adobe Illustrator or Microsoft Excel. These applications provide robust features for data visualization and customization.

- Once you've finalized your chart or infographic in the other application, export it in a format compatible with InDesign, such as:

  - **Scalable Vector Graphics (SVG):** Ideal for charts and infographics with vector elements as it maintains quality when scaled.

  - **Portable Network Graphic (PNG):** A common image format with good compatibility, but edits to the chart itself might require going back to the original application.

2. Placing and Editing Exported Files:

- In InDesign, use the **Place** function (File > Place) to import the exported SVG or PNG file containing your chart or infographic.

- Once placed, you can resize and position the chart within your layout using the Selection tool.

- InDesign offers limited editing capabilities for placed images. You can adjust brightness, contrast, or colour balance of the entire chart/infographic, but not individual elements within it.

3. Basic InDesign Tools (Limited Use):

- InDesign offers basic shape tools (rectangles, circles, lines) and the ability to fill them with colours or gradients. While not ideal for complex charts, you can create very simple bar charts or graphs for basic data representation.

- You can manipulate these shapes using the Pathfinder panel (similar to Illustrator) to perform elementary boolean operations (uniting, excluding, intersecting) to create more intricate shapes for charts.

Best Practices and Considerations:

- **Plan and Design Before Placing:** It's recommended to design your charts and infographics in a dedicated application like Illustrator for maximum control and customization.

- **Maintain Link with Original File (Optional):** If you plan on editing the chart data or design later, consider placing the SVG file as a linked asset. This ensures updates in the original application (e.g., Illustrator) are reflected in your InDesign document.

- **Consider Complexity:** For highly complex charts or infographics, avoid using InDesign's basic tools. It's better to create them in a more suitable application and place them in InDesign.

Additional Tips:

- Explore online resources and InDesign templates that might offer pre-designed charts and infographic elements you can incorporate into your layouts.

- If you need extensive chart creation capabilities alongside InDesign, consider integrating other Adobe applications like Illustrator or using third-party data visualization tools.

By understanding these methods and limitations, you can effectively add charts and infographics to your InDesign projects, enhancing data presentation and visual communication within your layouts.

8.3 Data Merge and Dynamic Content

InDesign's data merge feature allows you to import and integrate variable data from external sources into your document layout, creating multiple versions with unique content. This can be a powerful tool for generating personalized documents, product catalogues, or reports.

Here's a breakdown of the data merge workflow:

1. **Data Source Preparation:**

- You'll need your variable data in a structured format, typically a spreadsheet (.csv or .xlsx) created in Microsoft Excel, Google Sheets, or a similar program.

- Each column in the spreadsheet represents a field of variable data you want to insert into your InDesign document. The first row usually contains header labels for each data field (e.g., "Name," "Address," "Email").

2. **InDesign Document Setup:**

- Create your InDesign document with placeholder text frames, image frames, or other elements where you want the variable data to be inserted.

3. **Data Merge Panel:**

- Go to **Window > Utilities > Data Merge**. This opens the data merge panel.

- Click the **Select Data Source** button and choose your prepared spreadsheet file.

4. **Mapping Data Fields:**

- InDesign will import the data source and display the field names.

- Drag and drop each data field name (from the data source) onto its corresponding placeholder text frame or image frame within your InDesign document. This creates a link between the data field and the placeholder element.

5. **Preview and Generate:**

- Use the **Preview** button in the data merge panel to see how your document will look with different data records from your spreadsheet.

- Once satisfied, click **Merge** to generate multiple versions of your document, each with unique data populated from your spreadsheet.

Dynamic Content and Personalization:

- Data merge enables dynamic content, where elements in your layout change based on the imported data.

- This can be used for various applications:

  - **Personalized Marketing Materials:** Create customized brochures or flyers with recipient names and targeted messages.

  - **Product Catalogues:** Generate variations of product pages with specific product details and images pulled from your data source.

  - **Reports with Dynamic Data:** Populate reports with charts or text that update based on imported data sets.

Additional Considerations:

- **Data Cleaning and Formatting:** Ensure your data source is clean and formatted consistently to avoid errors during the merge process.

- **Sorting and Filtering (Limited):** InDesign offers basic options to sort or filter your data set within the data merge panel for focused generation of document variations.

- **Complex Layouts:** For intricate layouts with conditional formatting based on variable data, consider using Adobe InDesign Server, a paid service with advanced data merge capabilities.

By mastering data merge, you can streamline your workflow and create personalized or data-driven InDesign documents, saving time and effort compared to manually creating individual versions for each data set.

CHAPTER NINE

COLOUR AND EFFECTS

9.1 Colour Management and Swatches

InDesign's colour management and swatch system work together to ensure consistent and predictable colour output across different devices and printing processes. Here's a detailed breakdown of both aspects:

Colour Management:

- **Importance:** Colour management plays a crucial role in maintaining accurate colour representation throughout your design workflow. It ensures colours displayed on your screen closely match the final printed output or how they appear on other devices.

- **InDesign's Role:** InDesign provides tools to calibrate your monitor, set up colour profiles, and convert colours between different colour spaces (e.g., RGB for screen display, CMYK for printing) to maintain consistency.

- **Workflow:**

  1. **Calibrate Your Monitor:** Regularly calibrate your monitor using a hardware calibration tool to ensure it displays colors accurately.

  2. **Set Up Colour Settings:** Go to **Edit > Colour Settings**. Here, you can choose a preset based on your workflow (e.g., General Purpose for basic printing, Prepress for high-end printing). You can also define custom settings for specific printing processes.

3. **Colour Profile Embedding:** When placing images or importing graphics, ensure they embed ICC colour profiles. This helps InDesign interpret the colours accurately within your document.

Swatches Panel:

- **Organization and Consistency:** The Swatches panel serves as a central location to define, store, and reuse colours throughout your InDesign document. It helps maintain colour consistency and simplifies editing if you need to modify a colour later.

- **Creating Swatches:**
  - There are several ways to create swatches:
    - **From Existing Colours:** Select an object with the desired colour and click the **Create New Swatch** button in the Swatches panel.
    - **Define Colour Values:** Click the **New Colour Swatch** button and define the colour using various modes (e.g., CMYK, RGB, Lab) or by entering specific colour values.
    - **Import Swatches:** You can import swatch libraries from other InDesign documents or Adobe applications (like Illustrator) to share colour palettes across projects.

- **Swatch Types:**
  - InDesign supports various swatch types:

- **Process Colours:** Ideal for screen display and printing with standard process inks (CMYK).

- **Spot Colours:** Used for specific pre-mixed inks that may not be achievable with CMYK printing.

- **Gradients:** Define and store multi-colour gradients for fills and strokes.

- **Benefits of Using Swatches:**

  - **Consistency:** Ensures all instances of a particular colour use the same swatch, maintaining uniformity throughout your design.

  - **Easy Editing:** If you decide to change a colour, you can modify the master swatch, and all elements referencing that swatch will update automatically.

  - **Communication:** Sharing swatch libraries with printers or collaborators ensures everyone is using the same colour definitions.

Working Together:

By effectively utilizing colour management and the Swatches panel, you can achieve:

- **Colour Accuracy:** Maintain consistent colour appearance between your design on screen, printed output, and across different devices.

- **Efficiency:** Streamline your workflow by managing colours centrally and making edits efficiently.

- **Professional Results:** Deliver high-quality InDesign documents with predictable and professional-looking colour palettes.

Remember, colour management can involve technical aspects. Don't hesitate to consult additional resources or professional printers if you have specific colour requirements for your InDesign projects.

9.2 Applying Effects: Shadows, Gradients, and Transparency

InDesign offers a variety of effects that can elevate the visual appeal of your document and add depth and dimension to your design elements. Here's a closer look at three commonly used effects: shadows, gradients, and transparency.

1. Drop Shadows:

- **Adding Depth:** Drop shadows create the illusion of depth by simulating light hitting an object and casting a shadow behind it.

- **Customizing Shadows:** You can adjust various shadow properties like:

  - **Offset:** The distance of the shadow from the object.

  - **Blur:** The softness or crispness of the shadow edges.

  - **Colour:** The colour of the shadow (typically a darker shade of the object's fill colour).

  - **Angle:** The direction from which the light source is positioned, influencing the shadow direction.

- **Applying Drop Shadows:**

  - Select the object you want to add a shadow to.

  - Go to the **Effects** panel (Window > Effects).

  - In the **Object** dropdown menu, choose **Drop Shadow**.

  - Adjust the shadow properties in the settings panel and click **OK**.

2. Gradients:

- **Creating Visual Interest:** Gradients allow you to blend two or more colours smoothly within an object's fill or stroke, adding visual complexity and depth.

- **Customizing Gradients:** You can define the gradient using the Gradient panel (Window > Gradient). Here you can:

  - Choose gradient presets or create custom blends.

  - Set the start and end colours of the gradient.

  - Adjust the angle and direction of the colour transition.

  - Add multiple colour stops for more complex gradients.

- **Applying Gradients:**

  - Select the object you want to apply a gradient to.

  - In the **Fill** or **Stroke** panel (depending on where you want the gradient), click the coloured box next to the fill type (e.g., Solid).

  - Choose **Gradient** from the options and customize the gradient properties using the Gradient panel.

3. Transparency:

- **Controlling Opacity:** Transparency allows you to control the visibility of an object through varying degrees of opacity.

- **Applications:** Transparency can be used for various purposes, such as:

  - Creating overlays and subtle effects.

  - Layering objects with partial transparency for a more visually engaging design.

  - Simulating realistic textures and materials (e.g., glass effect).

- **Adjusting Transparency:**
    - o Select the object you want to adjust transparency for.
    - o In the **Appearance** panel (Window > Appearance), locate the **Fill** or **Stroke** section (depending on where you want to apply transparency).
    - o Reduce the **Opacity** value (percentage) to increase transparency. A value of 100% is fully opaque, while 0% is completely transparent.

Additional Tips:

- Experiment with different effect combinations to achieve unique visual styles.

- Use effects subtly to avoid overwhelming your design.

- Consider the hierarchy of your elements; prioritize clear communication with appropriate use of effects.

- Preview your effects at different zoom levels to ensure they appear as intended.

By mastering these effects and using them strategically, you can enhance the visual impact of your InDesign documents and create a more professional and engaging design experience.

9.3 Colour Separations and Printing Considerations

InDesign doesn't directly handle the printing process itself, but it provides crucial features for preparing your document for professional printing. A key aspect of this preparation is understanding colour separations and setting up your document accordingly.

Colour Separations:

- In commercial printing, most presses use a four-color process (CMYK) to reproduce a wide range of colours.

- CMYK stands for Cyan, Magenta, Yellow, and Black. The printing press lays down these inks in varying degrees to create the final colours on the printed page.

- To achieve this, your document needs to be separated into these four ink channels. Each channel represents the amount of a specific ink needed to create the final colours in your design.

Setting Up for Printing:

- **Document Profile:** Choose an appropriate colour profile for your printing process. InDesign offers presets like "US Web Coated (SWOP)" for standard coated paper stock.

- **Swatches:** Use a combination of process colours (CMYK) and spot colours for specific elements. Spot colours use pre-mixed inks that may not be achievable with CMYK printing.

- **Trapping (Optional):** For high-resolution printing, especially on absorbent paper, consider adding trapping to prevent thin gaps between colours (especially along edges) that might appear during the printing process. Trapping involves slightly overlapping colors to ensure a clean and professional outcome. Consult your printer for specific trapping recommendations.

Previewing Separations:

- InDesign's **Separations Preview** (Window > Output > Separations Preview) is a valuable tool to visualize how your colours will separate into CMYK channels.
- This allows you to identify potential issues like unexpected colour shifts or overprinting errors before sending your document to print.

Additional Printing Considerations:

- **Bleeds and Marks:** If your design elements extend to the edge of the final printed piece, set up bleeds in your InDesign document. Bleeds provide extra content beyond the cut line to account for minor trimming variations during printing. Printers often also require specific printing marks (trim marks, registration marks) to be added to your document for accurate cutting and assembly.
- **Resolution of Images:** Ensure all placed images in your InDesign document have a resolution that meets your printer's requirements. Typically, 300 dpi (dots per inch) is considered standard for high-quality printing.
- **Font Embedding:** If you're using non-standard fonts, embed them in your InDesign document to ensure the printer has access to the fonts used in your design.

Working with a Printer:

- It's always recommended to establish clear communication with your chosen printing service provider. Discuss your project requirements, paper stock choice, and any specific printing preferences.

- Your printer can advise on specific settings, colour profiles, and potential challenges based on your project and their printing equipment.

By understanding colour separations, setting up your InDesign document correctly, and collaborating with your printer, you can ensure a smooth printing process and achieve high-quality results for your InDesign projects.

CHAPTER TEN

OUTPUT AND PRINTING

10.1 Preflighting and Checking Document Errors

InDesign's Preflight panel acts as a quality assurance checkpoint before you send your document off for printing, publishing, or sharing. It meticulously examines your InDesign file for potential errors or inconsistencies that could lead to problems during output or down the line. Here's a breakdown of what Preflight does and how to use it effectively:

What Preflight Checks For:

- **Missing Fonts:** Identifies any fonts used in your document that are not embedded or available on the system where the document will be opened. Missing fonts can result in text appearing incorrectly.

- **Missing Links:** Checks for any linked images or graphics (e.g., EPS, JPG) that are missing from their designated locations. Missing links will result in empty image frames or placeholder text.

- **Low-Resolution Images:** Highlights images with resolutions below a specified threshold, which might appear blurry or pixelated in print.

- **Colour Issues:** Warns about potential colour problems, such as using spot colours in a CMYK printing process or colours outside the printable gamut.

- **Overset Text:** Identifies text frames where the text overflows the visible area, potentially getting cut off during output.

- **Object Attributes:** Checks for potential issues with object properties like transparency settings, effects, or overprinting elements, which might not translate well depending on the output format.

Using the Preflight Panel:

1. **Accessing Preflight:** Go to **File > Preflight** (or use the shortcut Ctrl/Cmd + Alt + F).

2. **Choosing a Profile:** InDesign offers various pre-configured Preflight profiles for different output scenarios (e.g., Basic Preflight for common checks, High Quality Print for stricter printing requirements). You can also create custom profiles.

3. **Running the Preflight Check:** Click the **Preflight** button. InDesign scans your document and displays a report listing any identified errors or potential problems.

4. **Addressing Errors:** The report categorizes errors and provides details about each issue. Double-clicking an error entry often takes you directly to the element in your document where the problem resides. You can then fix the issue and re-run Preflight to ensure a clean bill of health.

Benefits of Using Preflight:

- **Catching Errors Early:** Preflight helps identify potential issues before you export your document, saving time and effort compared to fixing problems after the fact.

- **Ensuring Quality Output:** By addressing preflight warnings, you can increase the chances of a successful print run or error-free digital delivery of your InDesign project.

- **Maintaining Consistency:** Preflight helps maintain consistency across your documents by identifying potential inconsistencies in fonts, colours, or object settings.

Additional Considerations:

- **Customize Preflight Profiles:** If you have specific output requirements, consider customizing a Preflight profile to tailor it to your needs.

- **Not a Foolproof Solution:** While Preflight is a powerful tool, it doesn't catch everything. It's still important to thoroughly review your document yourself before finalizing it.

- **Third-Party Plugins:** Several third-party plugins for InDesign offer additional preflight checks and functionalities.

By incorporating Preflight into your InDesign workflow, you can gain valuable peace of mind knowing your documents are thoroughly checked for potential errors before sending them off for further processing or sharing. It's a crucial step for professional output and maintaining high-quality standards for your InDesign projects.

10.2 Packaging Files for Print

Here's a detailed guide on packaging InDesign files for print, ensuring a smooth and error-free handover to your printing service provider:

Preparing Your InDesign Document:

- **Double-Check Document Errors:** Utilize InDesign's Preflight panel (Window > Preflight) to identify and address any potential issues like missing fonts, low-resolution images, or colour inconsistencies. Preflight helps ensure your document is technically sound for printing.

- **Review Bleeds and Marks:** If your design elements extend to the edge of the finished product, ensure you've set up bleeds in your document. Bleeds provide extra content beyond the cut line to account for minor trimming variations during printing. Additionally, include necessary printing marks (trim marks, registration marks) as instructed by your printer.

Collecting Required Files:

- **Fonts:** In most cases, you'll need to embed the fonts used in your document within the InDesign package. This ensures the printer has access to the exact fonts you used, preventing font substitution issues. You can find font embedding options within the Fonts panel (Window > Type > Fonts).

- **Linked Images:** All linked images (e.g., JPG, EPS, TIFF) referenced in your InDesign document need to be included in the package. Verify that none of the linked images are missing.

Creating the InDesign Package:

1. Go to **File > Package**.

2. In the **Package** window, you'll see a summary of your document information and a list of fonts and linked files.

3. **Destination Folder:** Choose a designated folder to save the packaged files.

4. **Package Options:** Here you can define what to include in the package. Ideally, select options to include:

   - ○ **Document:** The InDesign document itself (INDD file).

   - ○ **Fonts:** Embed all fonts used in the document.

   - ○ **Links:** Include all linked image files.

5. **Printing Instructions (Optional):** You can optionally add specific printing instructions within the package for your printer's reference.

6. Click **Package**. InDesign will create a new folder at the specified location containing your InDesign document (INDD file), a Fonts folder with all embedded fonts, and a Links folder with all linked images.

Additional Considerations:

- **Zipping the Package (Optional):** While not strictly necessary, consider compressing the entire package folder into a ZIP archive for easier sharing with your printer, especially if sending via email.

- **Communicate with your Printer:** It's always recommended to discuss your project requirements and any specific file delivery preferences with your printing service provider beforehand. They might have additional recommendations or require specific file formats for certain elements.

By following these steps and maintaining clear communication with your printer, you can ensure a seamless file handover process for your InDesign projects destined for print production.

CHAPTER ELEVEN

ADVANCED TECHNIQUES AND TIPS

11.1 Keyboard Shortcuts

Here's the rewritten version of the application menu for InDesign, with a more concise format:

- Preferences... | ⌘ + K | Ctrl + K | Opens the InDesign preferences window

File

- New: Document... | ⌘ + N | Ctrl + N | Creates a new document
- Open... | ⌘ + O | Ctrl + O | Opens an existing document
- Close | ⌘ + W | Ctrl + W | Closes the current document
- Save | ⌘ + S | Ctrl + S | Saves the current document
- Save As... | ⇧ + ⌘ + S | ⇧ + Ctrl + S | Saves the current document with a new name
- Place... | ⌘ + D | Ctrl + D | Places an image or file into the document
- Print... | ⌘ + P | Ctrl + P | Opens the print dialog
- Exit | (Quit on macOS) | (Exit on Windows) | Closes InDesign

Edit

- Undo | ⌘ + Z | Ctrl + Z | Undoes the last action

- Redo | ⇧ + ⌘ + Z | ⇧ + Ctrl + Z | Redoes the last undone action

- Cut | ⌘ + X | Ctrl + X | Cuts the selected text or object

- Copy | ⌘ + C | Ctrl + C | Copies the selected text or object

- Paste | ⌘ + V | Ctrl + V | Pastes the copied or cut content

- Select All | ⌘ + A | Ctrl + A | Selects all text or objects in the document

- Find/Change... | ⌘ + F | Ctrl + F | Opens the Find and Replace dialog

Layout

- Pages: Go to Page... | ⌘ + J | Ctrl + J | Opens the Go to Page dialog

- Pages: Add Page | ⇧ + ⌘ + P | ⇧ + Ctrl + P | Inserts a new page

- Pages: Delete Page | (Right-click on a page and select "Delete Page") | (Right-click on a page and select "Delete Page") | Deletes the selected page

- Margins and Columns... | ⌘ + M | Ctrl + M | Opens the Margins and Columns dialog

Type

- Character Styles | (Panel Menu) | (Panel Menu) | Apply or edit character styles

- Paragraph Styles | (Panel Menu) | (Panel Menu) | Apply or edit paragraph styles

- Insert Special Character... | Various shortcuts | Various shortcuts | Inserts special characters like hyphens, em spaces, etc.

Object

- Arrange: Bring to Front | ⇧ + ⌘ +] | ⇧ + Ctrl +] | Brings the selected object to the front

- Arrange: Send to Back | ⌘ + [| Ctrl + [| Sends the selected object to the back

- Group | ⌘ + G | Ctrl + G | Groups selected objects

- Ungroup | ⇧ + ⌘ + G | ⇧ + Ctrl + G | Ungroups a grouped object

- Transform: Move... | ⇧ + ⌘ + M | ⇧ + Ctrl + M | Opens the Transform dialog to move or rotate objects

View

- Zoom In | ⌘ + = or ⌘ + Num + | Ctrl + = or Ctrl + Num + | Zooms in on the document

- Zoom Out | ⌘ + - or ⌘ + Num - | Ctrl + - or Ctrl + Num - | Zooms out on the document

- Fit Page in Window | ⌘ + 0 | Ctrl + 0 | Makes the entire page fit within the window

- Fit Spread in Window | ⌥ + ⌘ + 0 | Alt + Ctrl + 0 | Makes the entire spread fit within the window

- Hide Rulers | ⌘ + R | Ctrl + R | Hides the rulers

- Show Grid | ⌘ + ' | Ctrl + ' | Shows the document grid

Window

- Arrange: Minimize | ⌘ + M or Ctrl + ⌘ + M | Ctrl + M or Ctrl + Ctrl + M | Minimizes the InDesign window

- Close | (Click the close button on the window) | (Click the close button on the window) | Closes the InDesign window

Note: This is not an exhaustive list of all InDesign shortcuts and menu options.

11.2 Collaboration and Sharing Tools

Collaboration and sharing tools are software applications that allow multiple people to work on a project together, even if they are in different locations. These tools can be essential for increasing productivity, improving communication, and ensuring everyone is on the same page. Here are some of the most common types of collaboration and sharing tools:

- **Document collaboration tools:** These tools allow multiple users to edit a document simultaneously. Popular examples include Google Docs, Microsoft Word Online, and Dropbox Paper.

- **Project management tools:** These tools help teams stay organized and on track by providing features like task lists, deadlines, and communication channels. Popular examples include Asana, Trello, and Monday.com.

- **File sharing tools:** These tools allow users to share files with each other easily and securely. Popular examples include Dropbox, Google Drive, and OneDrive.

- **Communication tools:** These tools allow teams to communicate with each other in real-time. Popular examples include Slack, Microsoft Teams, and Zoom.

- **Video conferencing tools:** These tools allow teams to see and hear each other in real-time, which can be helpful for meetings and brainstorming sessions. Popular examples include Zoom, Google Meet, and Microsoft Teams.

The best collaboration and sharing tools for you will depend on your specific needs and preferences. Consider factors such as the size of your team, the type of work you do, and your budget.

Congratulations on Completing This Book!

Well done on reaching the end! I hope this book has been insightful and valuable to you. May the knowledge and inspiration you've gained serve you well in your journey ahead. Wishing you success, growth, and all the best in your future endeavors!